REPORT

ON THE

RESOURCES OF THE UNITED STATES,

PRESENTED

TO THE INTERNATIONAL STATISTICAL CONGRESS AT BERLIN,

BY THE

HON. SAMUEL B. RUGGLES.

REPORT

IN RELATION TO THE

INTERNATIONAL AGRICULTURAL EXHIBITION

AT

HAMBURG, IN 1862.

BY

HON. JOSEPH A. WRIGHT.

WASHINGTON:
GOVERNMENT PRINTING OFFICE.
1864.

IN THE SENATE OF THE UNITED STATES, *January* 26, 1864.

Resolved, That fifteen hundred copies of the message of the President, communicating the report of Hon. Joseph H. Wright, Commissioner to the International Exhibition held at Hamburg, and of the report of the Secretary of State, communicating the report of Hon. Samuel B. Ruggles on the resources of the United States, presented to the International Statistical Congress at Berlin, be printed for the use of the Senate.

MESSAGE

FROM THE

PRESIDENT OF THE UNITED STATES,

TRANSMITTING

Report of Hon. Joseph A. Wright, in relation to the International Agricultural Exhibition at Hamburg in 1862.

Gentlemen of the Senate and House of Representatives:

In accordance with a letter addressed by the Secretary of State, with my approval, to the Hon. Joseph A. Wright, of Indiana, that patriotic and distinguished gentleman repaired to Europe and attended the International Agricultural Exhibition held at Hamburg last year, and has, since his return, made a report to me, which it is believed cannot fail to be of general interest, and especially so to the agricultural community. I transmit, for your consideration, copies of the letter and report. While it appears by the letter that no reimbursement of expenses or compensation was promised him, I submit whether reasonable allowance should not be made him for them.

ABRAHAM LINCOLN.

JANUARY 20, 1864.

DEPARTMENT OF STATE,
Washington, March 28, 1863.

SIR: You are aware that the President communicated to Congress, at its late session, an invitation from the government at Hamburg to the government and citizens of the United States to participate in an exhibition of agricultural products, machinery, and the like, which is to be held in or near that city in the course of next summer. No appropriation, however, was made to defray the expenses of any such participation on our part, nor was any authority granted upon the subject. The reasons for this need not be adverted to. They will easily occur to a gentleman of your experience in public life. The apparent indifference of Congress, however, in regard to the matter, cannot reasonably be imputed to any insensibility in regard to whatever may tend to the advantage of the agricultural interests of the country, or to any coldness towards Hamburg itself, with which we are closely connected by commercial and other ties, and which we acknowledge to be a community with every title to respect.

Notwithstanding, however, this apparent neglect of Congress, the President is unwilling that the United States should be without any representative on the occasion referred to. Moved, therefore, by a regard for your character and standing at home, and particularly by the practical interest which, it is understood, you take in agricultural affairs, the President desires you to repair to the exhibition at Hamburg, and there take charge of the interests of such citizens of the United States as may become exhibitors on the occasion. It is to be distinctly understood, however, that no expense to the United States is to be occasioned by them, and that your own services will be gratuitous.

I have the honor to be, sir, your obedient servant,

WILLIAM H. SEWARD.

Hon. JOSEPH A. WRIGHT.

SIR: In the fulfilment of the duties assigned me, as commissioner of the United States to the International Agricultural Exhibition, held at Hamburg, in July last, I beg leave to submit the following report:

On my arrival at Hamburg, two weeks prior to the opening of the exhibition, with a view to the reception and proper management of American articles, which had been sent forward in considerable numbers, I found that the most ample arrangements had been made for holding the exhibition.

The extensive grounds (covering more than eighty acres) were laid off with great taste and liberality. Substantial sheds, halls, and buildings were erected for the accommodation of more than four thousand entries of stock. In addition to this, space admirably adapted for machinery of all kinds—locomotives, steam-engines, steam-ploughs, farm implements, mineral products, artificial manures, plants, trees, flowers, fruits, seeds, and all this, too, so beautifully arranged in the midst of the flags of more than forty nationalities, as to add to the comfort of the thousands assembled to witness this the first international exhibition in Northern Europe.

Eight of the States, to wit: New York, New Jersey, Massachusetts, Rhode Island, Illinois, Connecticut, Vermont, and Indiana, were represented by delegates from the States, or their agricultural societies, who were received with your commissioner with every token of respect and consideration which could have been desired for the representatives of our country.

Thirty-four nationalities were represented at the exhibition in their contributions, including, among other things, four thousand and one hundred of the finest horses, cattle, sheep, and swine, (several of the reigning sovereigns of Europe being numbered among the contributors.) The show of horses was over six hundred. Hanover received the highest praise for the speed, size, elegance, and strength of her horses. She also divided the honor with Great Britain in showing the best and purest blooded cattle.

More than one thousand persons were contributors and competitors in this national contest for superiority.

Three thousand machines and farm implements were contributed, and seventy-five steam-engines of every variety were used in operating the power and machinery. It was no show of mere art, painting, design, or fancy; but one of *substantials*, consisting mainly of stock and machinery.

The principal portion of the machinery came from Great Britain; none of which is more deserving of special attention than that of ploughing by steam.

Liberal prizes were offered by the committee. Several unsuccessful efforts having been made in our own country to plough by steam, these trials received the especial attention of all Americans present. Five ploughs were entered, cutting from three to four furrows at each course, in a highly satisfactory manner. I was convinced that if some modification could be made by which the expense attending the machinery for this operation could be materially diminished, the introduction of ploughing by steam could be easily effected, so as to be highly advantageous to the agricultural interests in many portions of the country. It is most manifest that steam is designed to play an important part in many of the branches of agriculture. In the opinion of your commissioner, we have not been sufficiently mindful of the progress made in Great Britain and other portions of Europe in the improvements of agricultural implements, brought about by the sharp competition of the English manufacturer for the European market.

We are content with our unparalleled success, and we may well say we are ahead of the nations of the Old World in machinery, in its adaptation to the wants of the people, in cheapness and utility, in the great labor-saving machines of the day—threshers, mowers, reapers, grain-cleaners, &c., &c. Yet a few days' witnessing the steam-ploughs and steam-machines in operation upon the national fair-ground at Hamburg would induce you to say we are behind many of them in the application of steam to agricultural work. Whatever the wants of the present day may be, the time is not far distant when many portions of our country will require this wonderful element, if we shall fully develop the hidden resources of our rich but diversified country. So important did the exhibition of the steam-plough appear, that a partial promise was procured from an eminent English firm to attend the first national agricultural exhibition held in the United States, with their steam-ploughing apparatus, if an invitation should be extended to competitors in this mode of ploughing.

Some two thousand sheep were exhibited, comprising nearly all of the best breeds of Europe. It is believed to have been the largest show of fine wooled sheep of modern times. The great nurseries of merinoes of Prussia, Saxony, and Silesia, were fully represented, and the exhibition was the more interesting from the fact that nearly all of the continental breeds were present, some of them extensively, embracing also the best stocks from England. It affords me great pleasure to state that George Campbell, of Westminster, Vermont, was most successful in competing with the premium on merinoes. He had three hundred and fifty competitors, yet he had awarded to him two first-class, and one second-class premium. His success was most gratifying, and the more so from the fact that the committee awarding to Mr. Campbell this well-deserved triumph were unanimous in their opinion, and each member composing the committee represented different nationalities. Mr. Campbell sold his sheep on the ground to Count Sherr Thoss, of Silesia, for five thousand dollars.

Governor Smith, of Vermont, makes the following appropriate allusions to this subject, in his late message: "In February last, the State agricultural society appointed the honorable Daniel Needham, the efficient secretary of the society, commissioner to attend and represent the interests of the State at the great international exhibition, then to be held at Hamburg, in Germany. Other States were represented at the exhibition by commissioners appointed under State authority; New York, Rhode Island, Massachusetts, New Jersey, Illinois, and, I think, Pennsylvania, were represented. Among other products taken by the commissioner for exhibition were twelve merino sheep, and I am happy to congratulate the State upon the success which attended the enterprise. In the list of competitors for prizes at the exhibition were two thousand sheep, representing the best flocks from all the German States, from France, England, and nearly all the countries of Central Europe. Against this strong competition, and contending against the natural prejudices existing against American products, Vermont won, at the hands of an able and impartial board of judges, the two first, and one second prize, for her sheep.

"The result of this to the sheep-breeding interests of Vermont can hardly be estimated. It was a great achievement, and is destined to give to America, and especially to Vermont, that which Europe has for so long a time almost exclusively enjoyed, the rich and valuable trade in stock-breeding sheep."

Already has the fruit of Mr. Campbell's triumph and Governor Smith's prediction been realized; merino sheep have been shipped from Vermont for Australia, and other distant countries. This trade bids fair to be one of great benefit, not only to Vermont, but to every section of the Union, as it will necessarily carry with it other articles and productions from our diversified country.

After a most thorough examination, trial, and practical test, before a committee of distinguished and competent gentlemen, representing eleven nationalities, and amidst a host of competitors, we maintained our complete ascendency in reaping machines, the greatest of labor-saving machines, in cutting the staff of man's life, bread.

The golden medal was awarded to C. H. McCormick, of Illinois, whose splendid reaper took the like reward at the London exhibition. This machine surpassed in elegance of workmanship any agricultural machine on the ground, while his working machine at the trial only more fully demonstrated and confirmed the superiority which he had so long maintained in Europe and in America. The second prize for a reaping machine was awarded to a citizen of New York.

Twenty-five medals and diplomas were awarded to American contributors, a list of which is herewith furnished; there was also a complimentary testimonial presented to each of the States represented, "a large and beautiful Hamburg flag." Although the contributions from the United States were few, in comparison with those of other countries, yet those present attracted great interest from the thousands who thronged the grounds, to whom our implements, household articles, and agricultural inventions, were generally unknown. A crowd could be found at all times examining the American contributions, and orders were given for duplicates of hundreds of them; those present were sold.

The great majority of our articles, especially our farm implements, are well adapted to the wants of Northern Europe, and the prices at which they are manufactured enables us to compete successively with foreign manufacturers. It is to be regretted that our people did not take more interest in this international exhibition. Never was there such an opening for American skill and industry. Here American manufacturers and mechanics had opened to them, in the *house of their friends*, the opportunity of presenting their inventions, skill and products, direct, and free from those embarrassments so frequently attending former exhibitions in other portions of Europe, surrounded by those who are bound to us by so many ties of friendship and consanguinity; those devoted, wherever they go, to agricultural pursuits; those who cultivate the immense agricultural districts stretching from the Rhine to the Danube, from the Baltic to the Mediterranean.

The exhibition of American machinery and implements received a great accession from a most liberal donation, from several of the leading German merchants, bankers and citizens, of the city of New York, including a complete assortment of agricultural implements. These, with the premium reaper, contributed by Mr. McCormick, in connexion with many other articles from other American contributors, are to form the *nucleus* of an *agricultural museum*, to be established in Hamburg. This I regard as the most gratifying result attending this international exhibition to American interests.

Several thousand dollars were subscribed before I left Hamburg for this object, and doubtless it will be carried out by the well known liberality of her citizens.

The establishment of this museum, or depot, opens for all time to come a place of deposit for American skill and products. Hamburg is the third city of trade and commerce in Europe. Hamburg is the key, not only to the great German mind, but the open door-way to more than one hundred and fifty millions of the people of northern Europe. With Hamburg we have rapid and almost daily communication, and it is difficult to estimate the advantage which will accrue to our mechanical skill and industry, our manufactures, our commerce and trade, by the location of a museum for their deposit in a city situate like Hamburg, whose merchant princes hold in their hands the immense trade of Prussia, Austria, Sweden, Denmark, portions of Russia and the Zollverein States. *Trade and commerce invariably bring together men whose interests are affected thereby; men will follow the fruits of their labor to market.*

The case of Worthington & Co., of Jackson, Michigan, illustrates most forcibly the prospect held out to American industry, at this great assembling of the men of labor. They sent forward one case of gardening and harvesting tools, of the value of twenty dollars; such was their beauty and utility, they were sold upon being opened, on the ground, for more than twice their value. There can be no doubt, if the small appropriation asked for at the last Congress had passed, so well calculated to call the attention of our people in time to this exhibition, thereby arousing a spirit of emulation, hundreds if not thousands of samples of our diversified mechanical inventions and manufacturing skill, would have been upon the ground, and the foundation laid for a trade of hundreds of thousands of dollars. No American could walk over the ground and witness for himself the crowd, and the articles on exhibition, without wishing for a larger number of our inventions and productions, to exhibit side by side with those around him; all seemed to regret we had not our substantial farm wagons and carts, our carriages and buggies, our horses of speed and strength, our large work-oxen, and other productions, to show the thousands thus assembled the growth, skill and energy of the men of the New World. It is not to be understood that the show of articles was not large and diversified; I doubt if such an exhibition of stock, machinery, and the productions of the earth, has been held during this century. More than five hundred ploughs alone were entered; also seeds, grains, grasses, and wines in great quantities, from every section; and the same is true of minerals, the forests, and the products of the soil. Everything was well calculated not only to induce men to study the comparative merits of the articles of various countries, but to give them enlarged and liberal views, *to elevate the men of toil, and to make labor attractive.* We have much to learn from abroad. All acknowledge the great benefits of our county, State, and national fairs; the holding of an international exhibition in our own country, at some early period, would be productive of great good. Interchange is progress; exclusiveness is ignorance.

Five hundred copies of the agricultural reports of the States and Patent Office were distributed, through the hands of gentlemen having in charge the agricultural interests of their respective countries, with the view of receiving like reports in return therefor. An assortment of fine seed wheat, oats, rye, &c., were presented to the undersigned from northern Europe, which will be distributed to the States represented at the exhibition, and Patent Office. These reports were carefully distributed, with the view of placing them in such portions of the country as were seeking for information in relation to the resources and character of our country.

In a commercial point of view, many advantages are anticipated from our connexion with this great international exhibition. But the strong sympathy which has been awakened, and the long existing friendship which has been strengthened, towards the people of the United States, by the interest manifested by the chief executive officer of the States collectively, and the several States, in their efforts to promote the agricultural industry of the world, will far outweigh, at a time like this, all other advantages.

It was most manifest that the great German empire, with which we formed an early treaty of friendship and commerce, and with which we have maintained unbroken relations of peace from the days of Washington, regard our troubles with intense solicitude.

The presence of the American delegates and our inventions and products on this occasion was well calculated not only to promote the material interests of both countries, but to bind together more closely the long existing peaceable relations.

We found everywhere an ardent sympathy for the restoration of law and order; for our triumph, for the unity of our country; this feeling was most manifest among the friends and relatives of our adopted citizens in the fatherland.

It was not thought possible that we could succeed in achieving any triumph at this exhibition in the present unhappy condition of our country. Hence there was a *moral power* attending our success, as it displayed most visibly the energy of our people, the resources of our country, the confidence in the future of our government, and was well calculated to cement more closely the bands of existing friendship.

The appointment of a commissioner, as well as those of the delegates of the several States, would have been insufficient to have enabled our country to be represented to any extent by contributions, which would be considered worthy of our position and dignity among our European neighbors, had it not been aided by a liberal subscription, amounting to near $5,000, to aid in defraying the expense for the freight and shipment of articles from the United States to Hamburg, by the well known benevolent citizens of New York and Philadelphia, a list of whom is herewith furnished. I trust this advance will be refunded by Congress. The citizens of the State of New York were aided in forwarding their contributions by a general appropriation from the State of one thousand dollars, and the principal express companies, as well as the Hamburg steamship company, deducted twenty-five per cent. from their tariff of charges in favor of all articles for the exhibition.

I desire to acknowledge the great assistance and valuable aid rendered by the delegations from the several States: Austin Baldwin, from the States of New York and Connecticut; Colonel Daniel Needham, of Vermont; Governor Dyer and Colonel Vial, of Rhode Island; Charles Flint, of Massachusetts; General Halsted and Stephen Condit, of New Jersey; and Consul Marsh, of Illinois. The labors of Mr. Baldwin at home in presenting this subject to our people are well known; to him are we greatly indebted for the interest taken by our people in this exhibition. I cannot close this report without mentioning the indefatigable exertions of James R. McDonald, a member of the executive committee at Hamburg. Mr. McDonald was for many years the acting consul of the United States at Hamburg, and a native of Vermont. From the commencement of this movement he has labored assiduously for our welfare; kind and attentive to the wants of his countrymen, omitting no opportunity to advance the interests of our citizens; and to him, more than to any other person, should the success attending the exhibition be attributed.

Finally, in submitting this report, no effort has been made to enter into a minute detail, but to present a general view of this great International Agricultural Exhibition, with a brief reference to those questions in which we are the most deeply interested. I had the pleasure of visiting, while in France, the great model school and farm at Greignore, also the celebrated sheep farm at Rambouillet, and the farm at Vaujours, near Paris, at which experiments are making from the night manures of the city. All these are under the control of the Emperor. The great school at Rothersdam, in England, of Messrs. Law & Gilbert, is conducted by private enterprise, and may be justly placed among the most practical institutions in the world. Governments and individuals seem to be making most strenuous efforts, both by experimental and practical tests, realizing the greatest benefits therefrom. One fact alone will demonstrate the truth of this assertion. At the celebrated school already referred to in England, one acre of ground has been made to yield sixty bushels of wheat, whilst a corresponding acre by its side could only be made to yield fifteen bushels without the named culture and manuring.

We trust that the interest taken by the head of our nation, and by the several States through their delegates and commissioners to the late great exhibition, will prove an additional link in the chain of progress, and shall not only be an incentive to our country to make more rapid strides in developing its great resources, but shall place her ere long side by side with those countries who have proven, to the fullest extent, all that the earth by culture and labor can effect.

I have the honor to be yours, most respectfully,

JOSEPH A. WRIGHT.

ABRAHAM LINCOLN,
President of the United States.

Premiums and rewards to the American Exhibitors at the Hamburg Fair, July, 1863.

George Campbell, of Westminster, Vermont, for 12 sheep—two first-class, and one second premium, $150; C. H. McCormick, of Chicago, Illinois, (reaper,) one large gold medal and diploma; Seymour, Morgan & Co., Brockport, New York, (reaper,) silver medal and diploma; Thompson & Avery, Tunckhannock, Pennsylvania, (threshing,) silver medal and diploma; John Kelsey, Yardleyville, Pennsylvania, (harrow,) bronze medal and diploma; John Van Derbelt, New York, (assorted agricultural implements,) medal and diploma; L. P. Rose, Detroit, Michigan, (hoes and forks,) bronze medal and diploma; J. W. Free, Goshen, Indiana, (fanning mill,) bronze medal and diploma; Solomon Hubbell, Unadilla, New York, (seed sower,) bronze medal and diploma; James A. Saxton, Canton, Ohio, (reaper,) bronze medal and diploma; Whittmore, Belcher & Co., Chicopee, Massachusetts, (ploughs and straw cutters,) bronze medal and diploma; R. H. Allen, New York, (agricultural implements,) bronze medal and diploma; Hall & Spiel, Pittsburg, Pennsylvania, (plough iron,) bronze medal and diploma; E. A. Tampton, Worcester, Massachusetts, (wood machine,) bronze medal and diploma; J. Redstone, Indianapolis, Indiana, (shingle machine,) bronze medal and diploma; William D. Windle & Co., New York, (domestic utensils,) bronze medal and diploma; H. G. Hotchkiss, Lyons, New York, (essential oils,) bronze medal and diploma; Hall & Parshall, Lyons, New York, (essential oils,) bronze medal and diploma; B. P. Johnson, Secretary New York N. S. Agricultural Society, Albany, New York, (seeds,) medal and diploma; Sylvanus R. Ward, New York, (anthracite coal,) medal and diploma; George Campbell, Vermont, (turnip cutter,) medal and diploma; B. M. Rhodes, Baltimore, Maryland, (turnip cutter,) medal and diploma; Duryea ——, New York, (mazena,) medal and diploma; J. Johnson & Co., New York, (washing machine,) medal and diploma.

Subscribers to the fund of the Hamburg exhibition, May, 1863.

A. A. Low, New York	$250
Henry G. Stebbins, New York	250
Hoyt Brothers, New York	250
A. T. Stewart, New York	250
Moses Taylor, New York	250
Phelps, Dodge & Co., New York	250
Benedict, Hall & Co., New York	250
Abraham Bell & Son, New York	250
Reeves & Hoyt, New York	250
James Brown, New York	250
Winslow, Lanier & Co., New York	250
Lockwood & Co., New York	250
Thorne, Watson & Butman, New York	250
Morris Ketchum, New York	250
Frederick M. Mass, New York	150
E. H. Miller, New York	100
Israel Corse, New York	100
M. Armstrong & Sons, New York	100
Livermore, Clews & Co., New York	100

Philadelphia subscriptions.

Jay Cook & Co., Philadelphia	$250
J. Edgar Thompson, Philadelphia	250
Boler & Co., Philadelphia	100
McKean, Vorce & Co., Philadelphia	100
H. C. Carey, Philadelphia	100

LETTER

OF

THE SECRETARY OF STATE,

COMMUNICATING,

In answer to a resolution of the Senate of the 14th instant, a copy of the report on the resources of the United States presented to the International Statistical Congress at Berlin, in September last, by the Hon. Samuel B. Ruggles.

DEPARTMENT OF STATE,
Washington, January 18, 1864.

I transmit to the Senate, in answer to their resolution of the 14th instant, a copy of the report on the resources of the United States presented to the international statistical congress at Berlin, in September last, by the Hon. Samuel B. Ruggles, together with a copy of his letter to the Department of State, transmitting the report.

WILLIAM H. SEWARD.

The SENATE *of the United States.*

Mr. Ruggles to Mr. Seward.

BERLIN, *September* 14, 1863.

SIR: In pursuance of your instructions accompanying the appointment of the undersigned as representative of the United States of America at the international statistical congress at Berlin, in September instant, he embarked for Europe in the first German steamer after receiving his commission, and reached Berlin, after some detention on the Atlantic, on the afternoon of the 6th of September. No business of importance had been transacted in the congress up to that time, except the presentation of the credentials of the delegates.

On the 7th of September the credentials of the undersigned were presented and approved, at which time representatives from the following countries, stated in alphabetical order, had been duly admitted, viz:

The United States of America; Anhalt-Dessau; Austria; Baden; Bavaria; Belgium; the Danubian Provinces; Denmark; France; Frankfort; Great Britain; Hamburg; Hanover; Holland; Holstein; Hesse-Cassel; Hesse-Darmstadt; Italy; Lubeck; Mecklenburg-Schwerin; Norway; Oldenburg; Portugal; Prussia; Russia; Saxe-Coburg; Saxe-Weimar; Saxony; Spain; Sweden; Switzerland; Turkey; and Wurtemberg.

The representatives of most of the nations above specified made reports to the congress on the statistics of their respective countries, which will be duly published in German and in French, in the official proceedings or "*Compte Rendu*" of the congress. In general, the proceedings and debates were in the German language, but to some extent in French and English.

Through some accidental and unintentional omission, none of the states of South America, or of Central America, sent delegates to the congress, although Brazil, especially, had been represented in preceding sessions of the congress. The name of the undersigned was erroneously entered in the printed and published lists as delegate from "*North America*," but on his application the error will be corrected in the official report of the proceedings.

On Friday, the 11th of September, being the sixth day of the session, a statistical report was presented to the congress by the undersigned, in behalf of the United States of America, of which a copy is herewith transmitted.

It is proper to state that the composition and character of the congress, as shown by its proceedings and published reports at the preceding sessions, was merely "statistical," and in no respect economical or political, rendering it proper and necessary to refrain in the report from any speculations or deductions as to the practical use or employment of the resources to be statistically exhibited, or any political discussion of the character, conduct, or possible result of the pending insurrection against the government of the American Union; but rather to present the cardinal elements of its material strength and resources, past and present, in such arithmetical and statistical form as should furnish, of itself, to the congress and to the countries therein represented, sufficient elements for any necessary conclusions.

Again, it was desirable and necessary, for the purpose of securing the publication and circulation to any considerable extent, of such a statement, to condense the facts as far as practicable, to select only the most prominent, and to seek, by a well-defined outline, to present the subject clearly and distinctly.

Keeping these considerations in view, the report was therefore confined mainly to the four cardinal elements of our national strength, embraced under the heads—Territory; Population; Agricultural Production; and Preciuos Metals. It is not denied that other branches, though comparatively less important, might also have been added; but under the circumstances, those presented were thought sufficient for the present purpose.

In view of the insurrection still affecting the industry and products of a certain portion of the Union, and rendering it difficult to state or estimate their present value with any statistical accuracy, they were not embraced in the report to the present congress, under the belief that the full restoration of tranquillity before the next session, in 1865, will then enable the representative of the United States to fully supply the deficiency.

The present session has been signalized by the adoption of important resolutions in respect to a uniform system of weights, measures, and coins, for the use of the civilized world, and materially affecting the United States of America. A large commission, embracing representatives of high attainments from fourteen different nations and countries, was instituted at the congress of 1860, held in London, to report a system for consideration at the present session. The undersigned, on taking his seat in the body, was invited, in behalf of the United States, to confer and unite with that commission in its proposed and forthcoming report. A draught of that report had been printed, presenting, in review, the different nations which had adopted, or were disposed to adopt, the *metric* system of weights and measures, but in which it was stated that "the Confederate States of America have expressed a desire to introduce the metric system of weights and measures." The undersigned, on perceiving the statement, protested at once against its propriety, or its admission into the report, on the ground that "the Confederate States," so called, had no separate, national, lawful existence, but still formed integral portions of the United States of America. The objection was acquiesced in, and the words in question were modified so as to read, "Some of the States of America have expressed a desire," &c., &c. That statement is known to be true in respect to some of the States of South America, and possibly as to some of the States of our American Union.

The proposition presented by that commission to the congress in respect to weights, measures, and coins, looking to an eventual change in the weight of the British sovereign and of the American dollar, to reduce them to even multiples of the franc, with the modifications which these propositions underwent in the congress, are of so much importance and gravity, that the undersigned will require some little time for reporting them fully, with the necessary accompanying documents, to the government of the United States. He will seek to do so with all practicable despatch after his return to America. The subject necessarily embraces the grave and difficult question as to the relative value of gold and of silver, present and prospective, and the proper adjustment of the coins of both metals, to keep pace with the fluctuations in their production and supply. For this purpose, the undersigned thought it necessary to propose, at the conclusion of the report on the metalliferous regions of the United States, that the subject of the production of gold and silver should be investigated by a commission to be instituted by the international statistical congress; but on full consideration by the section to which the subject was referred, it was decided, and perhaps properly, that the investigation could not be properly made by the congress, which was statistical and not economical in its aims, and that the necessary inquiry might better be left to the governments of the three great gold-producing countries, being the United States, Great Britain in respect to Australia, New Zealand, and British America, and Russia; and more especially as the inquiry, to be of any practical value, must be conducted under the authority and direction of those respective governments. Meanwhile the decided opinion has been expressed by the delegates in the present congress from Great Britain and from Russia, that it may be reasonably expected that the necessary inquiries on a subject so important to the currency of the world will be prosecuted by those governments with all proper efficiency and despatch.

During the session of the present congress a resolution was passed, on motion of Professor Schubert, of the University of Konigsburg, that it was "advisable, and very useful to the general interests of statistical science, that of all official works and communications published by statistical bureaus, one copy shall be given to all the universities and high academies of the states of Europe, to be preserved in their libraries." A motion made by the undersigned, at a subsequent day, and seconded by Professor Schubert, was unanimously passed by the congress, that the resolution be modified and enlarged "so as to include the public libraries in *six* of the principal cities of the United States of America, to be designated by the State Department at Washington."

The congress adjourned on the 11th of September, after having received the marked hospitality and consideration of the government of Prussia, and of the inhabitants of Berlin.

Of the period of thirty days after the adjournment allowed to the undersigned for returning to the United States, he will employ the first two weeks in visiting Russia to collect the statistics of the product of gold in that country, and for which purpose the representatives of that government in the congress, and also the Russian minister at Berlin, have courteously afforded him important facilities.

The undersigned has the honor to remain, with high respect, your obedient servant,

SAMUEL B. RUGGLES.

His Excellency WILLIAM H. SEWARD,
Secretary of State, &c., &c., &c.

INTERNATIONAL STATISTICAL CONGRESS AT BERLIN.

Report from the United States of America.

Mr. Samuel B. Ruggles, delegate from the United States of America, presented the following report:

Mr. President and gentlemen of the International Statistical Congress:

The government of Prussia having specially requested, through its minister at Washington, his excellency the Baron Gerolt, that the government of the United States of America should send a representative to the international statistical congress to convene at Berlin on the 6th of September, 1863, the President of the United States, on the 14th of August, appointed the undersigned to that office. The session of the congress being so near at hand, the undersigned was necessarily obliged to embark for Europe without delay, and was thus prevented from collecting, in due season, as large a portion as could have been desired of the numerous documents and publications illustrating the statistics of the United States. Much important information, though often wanting in classification and arrangement, is embraced in various official papers issued under public authority, both national and State, and also by boards of trade and other voluntary societies whose labors are more or less statistical. Attempts have been made to impart to American statistics more of an analytical and scientific character, by means of official bureaus to be specially organized for the purpose. The State of Ohio, some years since, under the administration of Governor Chase, the present Secretary of the Treasury of the United States, established a Bureau of Statistics as one of the organs of the State government, which was committed to the charge of Mr. Mansfield, whose copious and instructive annual reports fully justify the selection; while far away in the remote interior, beyond the great chain of lakes, the infant State of Minnesota, with a single exception the youngest in the American Union, containing, by the census of 1860, but 173,000 inhabitants clustered around the headwaters of the upper Mississippi, and more than fifteen hundred miles from the Atlantic, established, almost at the moment of its birth, a Bureau of Statistics. Two of the annual reports of its able Commissioner of Statistics, Mr. Wheelock, are now submitted to the inspection of the international statistical congress, as affording reasonable ground of hope that, in due time, America may at least approach in scientific accuracy and philosophical arrangement the more mature and perfect performances of the statisticians of Europe.

The Congress of the United States has not yet established a distinct Bureau of Statistics, although repeatedly recommended and urged to do so; but in taking the census of inhabitants, as required by the national Constitution, at intervals not exceeding ten years, the practice has been gradually introduced of superadding, by special direction of Congress, inquiries more or less extensive in regard to various branches of industry and production, and recently embracing social statistics to a moderate extent; so that the Compend of the census of 1860, herewith submitted to the international statistical congress, will be found to contain a considerable mass of statistical information, illustrating the material, and, to some extent, the social and moral condition of the nation. Under the limited powers conferred by Congress, the active and intelligent officers who have successively filled the office of Superintendent, and particularly Mr. Kennedy, who participated in one or more of the previous sessions of the international statistical congress, have earnestly exerted their best efforts to render the inquiries authorized by law useful not only to the country, but to the cause of statistical science. It is confidently believed that the enlightened labors of the present body may do much to induce the legislative authorities of the United States to recognize a competent Bureau of Statistics as a national necessity, and thereby place their country on an equality, in that respect, with the most intelligent nations of the world.

Even then, some time must elapse before it will fully attain that power of acute, comprehensive, and thorough analysis in the various branches of statistical inquiry which has so distinguished the eminent European statisticians, in their valuable labors in the international statistical congress during the present and the preceding sessions.

It is a cause for general congratulation that those who conduct the public affairs of nations have become generally convinced that a state cannot be wisely or safely governed without an accurate knowledge of quantities. Abstract theories and historical traditions doubtless have their use and their proper place; but statistics are the very eyes of the statesman, enabling him to survey and scan with clear but comprehensive vision the whole structure and economy of the body politic—to adjust, in the finest harmony, all its varied functions—to regulate and invigorate the healthful circulation of every artery and vein, from the central, vital trunk, to the most remote and delicate articulation.

Not only so. In this modern world, where steam has abolished space, the statesman, to deserve the name, must carefully survey the statistics of all the nations that commerce can approach, so that, with nice and skilful hand, he may adapt the administration of his particular government to the due measure of its comparative capacities and powers.

It is under the conviction that this new-born, modern "solidarity of nations" renders the statistics of each important to all, that the undersigned, in behalf of the United States of America, now ventures briefly to invite the attention of the international statistical congress to some of the most prominent features exhibited by the Compend of the census of 1860, now before this body, and especially to the evidence which it furnishes of the rate and extent of material progress of the human race in that portion of the New World committed by Providence to the care of the American Union. The exhibition will certainly furnish, to some extent, the means of statistical comparison with other portions of the world, and thereby enable the international statistical congress in due time to discharge what may become a very important and world-wide duty, in classifying the results from the reports of individual countries, and thus to present in scientific form the prominent and distinctive features of the comparative anatomy of nations.

Nor is it to be feared that such a classification or comparison could ever be deemed useless or invidious. On this point the present body, fortunately, is able to refer to the highest authority. The impressive words in the opening address of the late Prince Albert, who deemed it no derogation from his eminent rank, as the royal consort of the British sovereign, to preside personally over your deliberations, and whose untimely death is mourned in both hemispheres as a loss to the human race, now come to us with solemn earnestness.

In the noble language of that truly exalted prince, such comparisons will only "prove to us afresh in figures, what we know already from feeling and experience—how dependent the different nations are upon each other for their progress—for their moral and material prosperity—and that the essential condition of their mutual happiness is the maintenance of peace and good will among each other. Let them be rivals, but rivals in the noble race of social improvement, in which, although it may be the lot of one to arrive first at the goal, yet all will equally share the prize—all feeling their own powers and strength increase in the healthy competition."

The Compend of the census of 1860, and other official documents now submitted to the international statistical congress, will establish the following cardinal facts in respect to the territory, population, and progress in material wealth of the United States of America:

I. The territorial area of the United States at the peace of 1783, then bounded west by the Mississippi river, was 820,680 square miles, about four times that of France, which is stated to be 207,145 exclusive of Algeria. The purchase from France of Louisiana, in 1804, added to this area 899,680 square miles. Purchases from Spain, and from Mexico, and the Oregon treaty with England, added the further quantity of 1,215,907 square miles; making the total present territory 2,936,166 square miles, or 1,879,146,240 acres.

Of this immense area, possessing a great variety of climate and culture, so large a portion is fertile that it has been steadily absorbed by the rapidly increased population. In May last there remained undisposed of, and belonging to the government of the United States, 964,901,625 acres.

To prevent any confusion of boundaries, the lands are carefully surveyed and allotted by the government, and are then granted gratuitously to actual settlers, or sold for prices not exceeding a dollar and a quarter per acre to purchasers other than settlers. It appears by the report of the Commissioner of the General Land Office, a copy of which is herewith furnished, that the quantity surveyed and ready for sale in September, 1862, was 135,142,999 acres. The report also states, that the recent discoveries of rich and extensive gold fields in some of the unsurveyed portions, are rapidly filling the interior with a population whose necessities require the speedy survey and disposition of large additional tracts. The immediate survey is not, however, of vital importance, as the first occupant practically gains the pre-emptive claim to the land after the survey is completed. The cardinal, the great continental fact, so to speak, is this: that the whole of this vast body of land is freely open to gratuitous occupation, without delay or difficulty of any kind.

II. The population of the United States, as shown by the census of 1860, was 31,445,080; of which number 26,975,575 were white, and 4,441,766 black, of various degrees of color—of the blacks, 3,953,760 being returned as slaves. Whether any or what proportion of the number are hereafter to be statistically considered as "slaves," depends upon contingencies, which it would be premature at the present time to discuss.

The increase of population since the establishment of the government has been as follows:

1790	3, 929, 827,			
1800	5, 305, 937,	increase	35.02	per cent.
1810	7, 239, 814,	"	36.45	"
1820	9, 638, 191,	"	33.13	"
1830	12, 866, 020,	"	33.49	"
1840	17, 069, 453,	"	32.67	"
1850	23, 191, 876,	"	35.87	"
1860	31, 445, 080,	"	35.59	"

This rate of progress, especially since 1820, is owing in part to immigration from foreign countries.

There arrived in the 10 years—

From 1820 to 1830	244, 490
From 1830 to 1840	552, 000
From 1840 to 1850	1, 558, 300
From 1850 to 1860	2, 707, 624
Total	5, 062, 414

Being a yearly average of 126,560 for the forty years, and 270,762 for the last ten years.

The disturbances in the United States caused by the existing insurrection and commencing in April, 1861, have temporarily and partially checked this current of immigration, but during the present year it is again increasing.

The records of the commissioners of emigration of New York show that the arrivals at that port alone have been, for—

	From Ireland.	From Germany.	Total, including all other countries.
1861	27,754	27,159	65,529
1862	32,217	27,740	76,306
1863, up to Aug. 20, 7⅔ months,	64,465	18,724	about.. 98,000

The proportions of the whole number of 5,062,414 arriving from foreign countries in the forty years from 1820 to 1860, were as follows:

From Ireland	967,366	
From England	302,665	
From Scotland	47,800	
From Wales	7,935	
From Great Britain and Ireland	1,425,018	
		2,750,784
From Germany	1,546,976	
From Sweden	36,129	
From Denmark and Norway	5,540	
		1,588,145
From France	208,063	
From Italy	11,302	
From Switzerland	37,732	
From Spain	16,245	
From British America	117,142	
From China (in California almost exclusively)	41,443	
From all other countries, or unknown	291,558	
		723,485
		5,062,414

It is not ascertainable how many have returned to foreign countries, but they probably do not exceed a million.

If the present partial check to immigration should continue, though it is hardly probable, the number of immigrants for the decade ending in 1870 may possibly be reduced from 2,707,624 to 1,500,000.

The ascertained average of increase of the whole population in the seven decades from 1790 to 1860, which is very nearly 33⅓ per cent., or one-third for each decade, would carry the present numbers (31,445,080) by the year 1870 to 41,926,750

From which deduct for the possible diminution of immigrants, as above 1,207,624

There would remain 40,719,126

Mr. Kennedy, the experienced Superintendent of the Census, in the Compend published in 1862, at page 7, estimates the population of 1870 at 42,318,432, and of 1880 at 56,450,241.

The rate of progress of the population of the United States has much exceeded that of any of the European nations. The experienced statisticians in the present congress can readily furnish the figures precisely showing the comparative rate.

The population of France in

1801 was	27, 349, 003
1821 was	30, 461, 875
1831 was	32, 569, 223
1841 was	34, 230, 178
1851 was	35, 283, 170
1861 was	37, 472, 132

Being about 37 per cent. in the sixty years. It does not include Algeria, which has a European population of 192,746.

The population of Prussia has increased since 1816 as follows:

1816	10, 319, 993
1822	11, 664, 133
1834	13, 038, 970
1840	14, 928, 503
1849	16, 296, 483
1858	17, 672, 609
1861	18, 491, 220

Being at the rate of 79 per cent. in forty-five years.

The population of England and Wales was, in

1801	9, 156, 171
1811	10, 454, 529
1821	12, 172, 664
1831	14, 051, 986
1841	16, 035, 198
1851	18, 054, 170
1861	20, 227, 746

Showing an increase of 121 per cent. in the sixty years, against an increase in the United States in sixty years of 593 per cent.

III. The natural and inevitable result of this great increase of population, enjoying an ample supply of fertile land, is seen in a corresponding advance in the material wealth of the people of the United States. For the purpose of State taxation, the values of their real and personal property are yearly assessed by officers appointed by the States. The assessment does not include large amounts of property held by religious, educational, charitable, and other associations exempted by law from taxation, nor any public property of any description. In actual practice, the real property is rarely assessed for more than two-thirds of its cash value, while large amounts of personal property, being easily concealed, escape assessment altogether.

The assessed value of that portion of property which is thus actually taxed increased as follows: In 1791 (estimated) $750,000,000; 1816 (estimated) $1,800,000,000; 1850 (official valuation) $7,135,780,228; 1860 (official valuation) $16,159,616,068, showing an increase in the last decade alone of $9,023,835,840.

A question has been raised, in some quarters, as to the correctness of these valuations of 1850 and 1860, in embracing in the valuation of 1850 $961,000,000, and in the valuation of 1860 $1,936,000,000, as the assessed value of slaves, insisting that black men are persons and not property, and should be regarded, like other men, only as producers and consumers. If this view of the subject should be admitted, the valuation of 1850 would be reduced to $6,174,780,000, and that of 1860 to $14,223,618,068, leaving the increase in the decade $8,048,825,840.

The advance, even if reduced to $8,048,825,840, is sufficiently large to require the most attentive examination. It is an increase of property over the valuation of 1850 of 130 per cent., while the increase of population in the same decade was but 35.99 per cent. In seeking for the cause of this discrepancy, we shall reach a fundamental and all-important fact which will furnish the key to the past and to the future progress of the United States. It is the power they possess, by means of canals and railways, to practically abolish the distance between the seaboard and the widespread and fertile regions of the interior, thereby removing the clog on their agricultural industry, and virtually placing them side by side with the communities on the Atlantic. During the decade ending in 1860 the sum of $413,541,510 was expended within the limits of the interior central group, known as the "food-exporting States," in constructing 11,212 miles of railway to connect them with the seaboard. The traffic receipts from those roads were—

In 1860	$31, 335, 031
In 1861	35, 305, 509
In 1862	44, 908, 405

The saving to the communities themselves in the transportation, for which they thus paid $44,908,405, was at least five times that amount, while the increase in the exports from that portion of the Union greatly animated not only the commerce of the Atlantic States, carrying those exports over their railways to the seaboard, but the manufacturing industry of the eastern States that exchange the fabrics of their workshops for the food of the interior.

By carefully analyzing the $8,048,825,840 in question, we find that the six manufacturing States of New England received $735,754,244 of the amount; that the middle, Atlantic, or carrying and commercial States, from New York to Maryland, inclusive, received $1,834,911,579; and that the food-producing interior itself, embracing the eight great States of Ohio, Indiana, Illinois, Michigan, Wisconsin, Minnesota, Iowa, and Missouri, received $2,810,000,000. This very large accession of wealth to this single group of States is sufficiently important to be stated more in detail. The group, taken as a whole, extends from the western boundaries of New York and Pennsylvania to the Missouri river, through fourteen degrees of longitude, and from the Ohio river north to the British dominions, through twelve degrees of latitude. It embraces an area of 441,167 square miles, or 282,134,688 acres, nearly all of which is arable and exceedingly fertile, much of it in prairie and ready at once for the plough. There may be a small portion adjacent to Lake Superior unfit for cultivation, but it is abundantly compensated by its rich deposits of copper and of iron of the best quality.

Into this immense natural garden, in a salubrious and desirable portion of the temperate zone, the swelling stream of population, from the older Atlantic States and from Europe, has steadily flowed during the last decade, increasing its previous population from 5,403,595 to 8,957,690, an accession of 3,554,095 inhabitants gained by the peaceful conquest of Nature, fully equal to the population of Silesia, which cost Frederick the Great the seven years' war, and exceeding that of Scotland, the subject of struggle for centuries.

The rapid influx of population into this group of States, increased the quantity of the "improved" land, thereby meaning farms more or less cultivated, within their limits, from 26,680,361 acres in 1850 to 51,826,395 acres in 1860, but leaving a residue yet to be improved of 230,308,293 acres. The area of

25,146,054 acres thus taken in ten years from the prairie and the forest is equa- to seven-eighths of the arable area of England, stated by its political economists to be 28,000,000 of acres.

The area embraced in the residue will permit a similar operation to be repeated eight times successively, plainly demonstrating the capacity of this group of States to expand their present population of 8,957,690 to at least thirty, if not forty, millions of inhabitants without inconvenience.

The effects of this influx of population in increasing the pecuniary wealth as well as the agricultural products of the States in question are signally manifest in the census. The assessed value of their real and personal property ascended from $1,116,000,000 in 1850 to $3,926,000,000 in 1860, showing a clear increase of $2,810,000,000. We can best measure this rapid and enormous accession of wealth by comparing it with an object which all nations value, the commercial marine. The commercial tonnage of the United States

In 1840 was ....2,180,764 tons.
In 1850 was ....3,535,454 "
In 1860 was ....5,358,808 "

At $50 per ton, which is a full estimate, the whole pecuniary value of the 5,358,808 tons, embracing all our commercial fleets on the oceans and the lakes and the rivers, and numbering nearly thirty thousand vessels, would be but $267,940,000; whereas the increase in the pecuniary value of the States under consideration, in each year of the last decade, was $281,000,000. Five years' increase would purchase every commercial vessel in the Christian world.

But the census discloses another very important feature, in respect to these interior States, of far higher interest to the statisticians and especially to the statesmen of Europe, than any which has yet been noticed, in their vast and rapidly increasing capacity to supply food, both vegetable and animal, cheaply and abundantly, to the increasing millions of the Old World. In the last decade their cereal products increased from 309,950,295 bushels to 558,160,323 bushels, considerably exceeding the whole cereal product of England, and nearly if not quite equal to that of France. In the same period the swine, who play a very important part in consuming the large surplus of Indian corn, increased in number from 8,536,182 to 11,039,352, and the cattle from 4,373,712 to 7,204,810. Thanks to steam and the railway, the herds of cattle who feed on the meadows of the upper Mississippi are now carried in four days, through eighteen degrees of longitude, to the slaughter-houses on the Atlantic.

It is difficult to furnish any visible or adequate measure for a mass of cereals so enormous as 558,000,000 of bushels. About one-fifth of the whole descends the chain of lakes, on which 1,300 vessels are constantly employed in the season of navigation. About one-seventh of the whole finds its way to the ocean through the Erie canal, which has already been once enlarged for the purpose of passing vessels of two hundred tons, and is now under survey by the State of New York, for a second enlargement, to pass vessels of five hundred tons. The vessels called "canal boats," now navigating the canal, exceed five thousand in number, and if placed in a line would be more than eighty miles in length.

The barrels of wheat and flour alone, carried by the canal to the Hudson river, were

In 1842..1,146,292.
In 1852..3,937,366
In 1862..7,516,397.

A similar enlargement is also proposed for the canal connecting Lake Michigan with the Mississippi river. When both the works are completed, a barrel of flour can be carried from St. Louis to New York, nearly half across the continent, for fifty cents, or a ton from the Iron mountain of Missouri for five dollars.

The moderate portion of the cereals that descends the lakes, if placed in barrels of five bushels each, and side by side, would form a line five thousand miles long. The whole crop, if placed in barrels, would encircle the globe. Such is its present magnitude. We leave it to statistical science to discern and truly estimate the future. One result is, at all events, apparent A general famine is now impossible; for America, if necessary, can feed Europe for centuries to come. Let the statesman and philanthropist ponder well the magnitude of the fact, and all its far-reaching consequences, political, social, and moral, in the increased industry, the increased happiness, and the assured peace of the world.

IV. The great metalliferous region of the American Union is found between the Missouri river and the Pacific ocean. This grand division of the republic embraces a little more than half of its whole continental breadth. Portland, in Maine, is the meridian 70° west from Greenwich; Leavenworth, on the Missouri river, in 95°; and San Francisco, on the Pacific, in 123°. By these continental landmarks the western or metalliferous section is found to embrace 28°, and the eastern division between the Missouri and the Atlantic, at Portland, 25° of our total territorial breadth of 53° of longitude.

It has been the principal work and office of the American people, since the foundation of their government, to carry the machinery of civilization westward from the Atlantic to the Missouri. the great confluent of the Mississippi. So far as the means of rapid intercommunication are concerned, the work may be said to be accomplished, for a locomotive engine can now run without interruption from Portland to the Missouri, striking it at St. Joseph, just below the fortieth parallel of latitude. In the twenty years preceding 1860, a network of railways 31,196 miles in length, was constructed, having the terminus of the most western link on the Missouri river. The total cost was $1,151,560,829, of which $850,900,681 was expended in the decade between 1850 and 1860.

The American government and people had become aware of the great pecuniary, commercial, and political results of connecting the ocean with the food-producing interior by adequate steam communications. But the higher and more difficult problem was then presented, of repeating the effort on a scale still more grand and continental; of winning victories still more arduous over Nature; of encountering and subduing the massive mountain ranges interposed by the prolongation of the Cordilleras of our sister continent through the centre of North America, rising, even at their lowest points of depression, far above the highest peaks of the Atlantic States.

The government, feeling the vital, national importance of closely connecting the States of the Atlantic and of the Mississippi with the Pacific with all practicable despatch, has vigorously exerted its power. On the 1st of July, 1862, nearly fifteen months after the outbreak of the existing insurrection, and notwithstanding the necessity of calling into the field more than half a million of men to enforce the national authority, Congress passed an act for incorporating "The Union Pacific Railway Company," and appropriated $66,000,000 in the bonds of the United States, with large grants of land, to aid the work, directing it to be commenced at the 100th meridian of longitude, but with four branches extending eastward to the Missouri river. The necessary surveys across the mountain ranges are now in active progress, and the construction of the eastern division leading westward from the mouth of the Kansas river, on the Missouri, has actually commenced. The whole of that division, including that part of the line west of the 100th meridian to the foot of the Rocky mountains, is on a nearly level plain, and is singularly easy of construction. Its western end will strike the most prominent point of the auriferous regions in the Territory of Colorado, where the annual product of gold, as stated in the official message of the territorial governor, is from five to ten millions of dollars. The gold is there extracted by crushing machines from the quartz, in which it is found extensively distributed, needing only the railway from the Missouri to cheaply carry the necessary miners with their machinery and supplies. The distance to that point will be about six hundred and fifty miles, which will be passed in twenty-eight hours. When completed, as it easily may be, within the next three years, it will open the way for such an exodus of miners as the country has not seen since the first discoveries in California, to which the American people rushed with such avidity, many of them circumnavigating Cape Horn to reach the scene of attraction.

Meanwhile, a corresponding movement has commenced on the Pacific, in vigorously prosecuting the construction of the railway eastward from the coast at or near San Francisco, which will cross the Sierra Nevada at an elevation of about 7,000 feet, on the eastern line of California, in the 120th parallel of longitude, and there descend into the Territory of Nevada at the rich silver mines of Washoe.

It is not yet possible to estimate with any accuracy the extent of these deposits of gold and silver, but they are already known to exist at very numerous localities in and between the Rocky mountains and the Sierra Nevada, not to mention the rich quartz mining regions in California itself, which continue to pour out their volumes of gold to affect, whether for good or ill, the financial condition of the civilized world. During the last six months gold has been obtained in such quantities, from the sands of the Snake river and other confluents of the Columbia river, as to attract more than twenty thousand persons to that remote portion of our metalliferous interior. The products of those streams alone for the present year are estimated at twenty millions of dollars.

The Commissioner of the General Land Office, in his official report of the 29th December, 1862, states as follows:

"The great auriferous region of the United States, in the western portion of the continent, stretches from the 49th degree of north latitude and Puget sound to the 30° 30′ parallel, and from the 102d degree of longitude west of Greenwich to the Pacific ocean, embracing portions of Dakota, Nebraska, Colorado, all of New Mexico, with Arizona, Utah, Nevada, California, Oregon and Washington Territories. It may be designated as comprising 17 degrees of latitude, or a breadth of eleven hundred miles from north to south, and of nearly equal longitudinal extension, making an area of more than a million square miles.

"This vast region is traversed from north to south, first, on the Pacific side, by the Sierra Nevada and Cascade mountains, then by the Blue and Humboldt; on the east, by the double ranges of the Rocky mountains, embracing the Wahsatch and Wind River chain, and the Sierra Madre, stretching longitudinally and in lateral spurs, crossed and linked together by intervening ridges, connecting the whole system by five principal ranges, dividing the country into an equal number of basins, each being nearly surrounded by mountains and watered by mountain streams and snows, thereby interspersing this immense territory with bodies of agricultural lands, equal to the support not only of miners, but of a dense population."

"These mountains," he continues, "are literally stocked with minerals; gold and silver being interspersed in profusion over this immense surface, and daily brought to light by new discoveries." "In addition to the deposits of gold and silver, various sections of the whole region are rich in precious stones, marble, gypsum, salt, tin, quicksilver, asphaltum, coal, iron, copper, lead, mineral and medicinal, thermal, and cold springs and streams."

"The yield of the precious metals alone of this region will not fall below one hundred millions of dollars the present year, and it will augment with the increase of population for centuries to come." "Within ten years the annual product of these mines will reach two hundred millions of dollars in the precious metals, and in coal, iron, tin, lead, quicksilver and copper, half that sum." He proposes to subject these minerals to a government tax of 8 per cent. and counts upon a revenue from this source of 25 millions per annum, almost immediately, and upon a proportionate increase in the future. He adds, that "with an amount of labor relatively equal to that expended in California applied to the gold fields already known to exist outside of that State, the production of this year, including that of California, would exceed four hundred millions." In a word," says he, "the value of these mines is absolutely incalculable."

From the documents and other evidences now before the International Statistical Congress, it must be apparent that the metalliferous regions of the United States of America are destined, sooner or later, to add materially to the supply of the precious metals and thereby to affect the currency of the word, especially if taken in connexion with the capacity of the auriferous regions of Russia, Australia, and British America, and the possibility of increased activity in the mines of Mexico.

The undersigned would therefore respectfully beg leave to conclude the present report with the suggestion, that a commission be instituted by the body now assembled, with authority to collect such facts as may be gathered from authentic sources, in respect to the probable future production of gold and silver, and to present them for consideration to the International Statistical Congress at the next or some future session.

S. B. RUGGLES.

BERLIN, *September* 11, 1863.

www.ingramcontent.com/pod-product-compliance
Lightning Source LLC
LaVergne TN
LVHW011147110826
845150LV00008B/2550
* 9 7 8 1 4 1 8 1 9 2 3 0 3 *